PERSONAL RELIGION AND THE LIFE
OF DEVOTION

PERSONAL RELIGION

AND

THE LIFE OF DEVOTION

BY

W. R. INGE

Dean of St. Paul's

WITH AN INTRODUCTION BY
THE LORD BISHOP OF LONDON

WITH FRONTISPIECE

LONGMANS, GREEN AND CO.
39 PATERNOSTER ROW, LONDON, E.C. 4
NEW YORK, TORONTO
BOMBAY, CALCUTTA AND MADRAS
1924

IN MEMORIAM FILIOLÆ DILECTISSIMÆ

Filia, non ullos obliviscenda per annos,
  dulce decus nostræ deliciæque domus,
quantulacumque meæ debentur tempora vitæ,
  nulla aderit sine te nox mihi, nulla dies.
nondum bis senos ætas tua viderat annos ;
  explesti spatio tempora longa brevi.
immatura quidem non imperfecta fuisti ;
  in te grande Deus deproperavit opus.
læta puellari solita es te iungere ludo,
  læta iocos hilares carpere, læta choros ;
sic tamen interdum ut te non latuisse putarem
  unde fores et qua mox reditura via ;
advena ceu nostris qui delectatur in oris,
  sed patriæ non vult immemor esse domus.
lenis erat cursus morbi, nec cœperat umquam
  tam cari capitis nos cruciare dolor ;
sed sensim vitæ compagine lassa solula
  submisit placida dulce quiete caput.
summa dies aderat, pictam cum mane tabellam
  attuleram extremo deposuique toro.
illa meum complexa caput, ' pater optime,' dixit,
  ' scisne, pater, quantum te tua filia amet ? '
at quæ marcentem docuit Deus ipse puellam,
  quam prope virgineo constitit ipse toro !
huc veluti sacras accedebamus ad aras ;
  hic dulcis pietas hic habitabat amor.

tu mihi testis eras, medice o carissime, tuque
  iuncta illi studio fida ministra pari.
nec fuit illa minus sociis dilecta puellis,
  accipere in coetum quae voluere suum.
his placet in ludo personas sumere fictas,
  induere et propria pallia facta manu.
Asphodeli nostram appellant cognomine Paulam ;
  nobilis affertur vestis et apta deae.
regina Elysii campi prodire iubetur ;
  tota cohors parvam rite salutat heram.
quam decuit macro ridentis fastus in ore,
  quam pulcre exsangues subrubuere genae !
e quibus una diu pictura clara sodalem
  ingenio voluit nobilitare suo.
pingitur in tabula caelo mea Paula recepta,
  narcissos praebet quae pudibunda Deo.
parvulus arridens Christus cum virgine matre
  porrigit infantes ad pia dona manus.
quem circumvolitat tenerorum coetus Amorum ;
  lucent caeruleo sidera multa polo.
infra vernat humus ; totum flaventibus agrum
  candida narcissis lilia mixta tegunt.
sic placet in caelum sumptam mihi fingere natam,
  cui fuerat cordi quidquid ubique nitet.
respice nos, si fas illic meminisse tuorum,
  aspectu frueris qua propiore Dei.
at, pater, immerito cui pascere contigit agnam
  in gremium qualem tollere Christus amat,
quod Dominus donavit et imputat accipe munus ;
  abreptam noli plangere ; disce sequi.

INTRODUCTION

I FEEL very grateful to the Dean of St. Paul's for writing this beautiful little book for us, and especially for unveiling his soul to us in the last chapter.

We were all with him in spirit and sympathy when he so bravely gave back his beloved little daughter to God just before last Easter, but it is not easy for a naturally reserved man to write about such a sorrow in order to help others, and I feel certain that his many readers throughout the world will be grateful to him for doing so. It will strengthen many mourners to learn that " bereavement is the deepest initiation into the mysteries of human life, an initiation more searching and profound than even happy love. Love remembered and consecrated by grief belongs, more clearly than the happy intercourse of friends, to the eternal world; it has proved stronger than death." (p. 88.)

But it is not only in the last chapter that the author of this book has revealed the secret of his own life. I well remember—and he will forgive my recalling it— an intimate conversation which I once had with him

on the deep things of faith and when I mentioned one
great movement of thought against the Christian faith,
he said at once, " That hits me *where I live*." Those
who have only read " Outspoken Essays " or even
the Dean's great work on " Plotinus " will have a
revelation in this book of *where the author lives*, and will
be led on—that is the object of having these books
written for Lent—into a kingdom of faith, hope, joy
and consecration which is " not of this world."

And yet while the book breathes, as we should expect,
the air of Christian Mysticism, I would call the reader's
attention to a valuable passage which refutes the idea
that the Christian Mystic leaves the present world to
look after itself. " Nothing can be more untrue than
to suppose that the progress of the kingdom of God
upon earth is not a matter of deep interest for true
Christians. When Christ said to His disciples, ' I have
taken you out of the world,' He certainly did not mean
that He had taken them out of human society, with
its duties and obligations. Heaven is not a far-away
place to which we hope to go ; it is the presence of
God in which we ought to live. The Christian soldier
is no recreant, tarrying behind at the base and leaving
others to go into the fighting line. And here comes
the partial truth which, as I said, is mixed with much
error in the popular cult of the corporate idea. We
do need another co-operative society to combat the

society of co-operative guilt which the New Testament calls the world. We must help each other to make the right life possible in society. This is the true office of the Church, the bonds of which Christ meant to be mutual love and willing service. In this sense, we do need to make Church life much more of a reality." (p. 85.)

I have quoted this passage in full, as it serves to remove a popular misrepresentation of Christian Mysticism. These Christian Mystics do "turn the world upside down" but largely by being what they are. It is *character* that tells all the world over, but it is not a selfish ambition they set before themselves; they make their own a sentence of their Lord's, quoted more than once in these chapters, "For *their sakes* I sanctify myself that they also may be sanctified in truth."

I hope that this book may find many readers on both sides of the Atlantic.

A. F. LONDON.

CONTENTS

PREFATORY NOTE

The first Chapter is reprinted, with permission, from the first number of *The Pilgrim*. Part of the Chapter on " Hope " formed one of the *National Mission Pamphlets*, and is reprinted with the permission of the Society for Promoting Christian Knowledge. The photograph is reproduced by permission of Charlton, Canterbury.

CHAPTER I

WHEN we say our prayers, we are sometimes only making petitions that something which we desire may be granted to us. Very often this kind of prayer is all that we can achieve. But prayer itself is the elevation of the mind to God, and we cannot pray unless we believe that the mind is capable of being so elevated. From time to time this belief receives confirmation by a consciousness that we are in communication with a world of spiritual reality which at other times is closed to us. The curtain which hangs between us and the unseen is not drawn aside, but streaks of light are plainly discerned from behind it, and we cannot doubt that we have stood for a while on the threshold of a great experience. These moments, which are among the most sacred in human life, are known to almost all who have formed the habit of prayer, though they are so much a matter of temperament that neither their frequency nor their intensity is any certain indication of proficiency in the spiritual life, or any proof that our lives are accepted by God.

It is not only in prayer that these glimpses into the world beyond the veil are granted to us. Whether we realise it or not, it is for this purpose that we love to leave the busy haunts of men, and to seek our recreation in lonely places, amid the scenes of unspoilt nature. On the mountain-top, where the air is pure and a wide prospect lies open before our eyes, we feel our kinship with the rest of creation ; and whether the scene is one of gentle beauty or of awful sublimity, our restless souls find peace and our covetous desires are stilled. An even stronger " purgation of the emotions " is effected by " the moving waters at their priest-like task of pure ablution round earth's human shores " : we can understand, as we watch the waves, how Euripides in his cell overlooking the Aegean came to write the line, " The sea can wash away all human ills." But here, even more than in prayer, we have to admit the widest differences of temperament. Many love Wordsworth, but few can see and feel nature as he did, in moments

> " when the light of sense
> Goes out, but with a flash that has revealed
> The invisible world."

There are many to whom nature is dumb, or to whom she only gives back their own thoughts, taking the colours, grave or gay, of their passing moods.

There are other initiations, which few are so unhappy as to miss entirely. Love, whether in its most exalted form as the love between husband and wife, or in the less ardent experience of affection and sympathy, unlocks the doors of our prison-house and reveals to us something of the breadth and length and depth and height of the spiritual world which surrounds us. In various degrees, all cordial human intercourse is a liberation and an enhancement of our personality ; it is a channel of revelation.

These are the different forms of the mystical experience, and the whole structure of what is called mysticism, whether as a philosophy or as a rule and discipline of life, is built upon this empirical foundation. The mystical sense is so far from being a rare endowment, or an abnormality which we may hesitate whether we should class as pathological, that it is, in one or other of its forms, almost universal. But it is only the few who either speculate about its origin and nature or try to penetrate further into its secrets. Those who have endeavoured to think out the meaning of the mystical experience, and to co-ordinate it with the rest of our knowledge, are the philosophical mystics; those who have tried to develop the faculty in themselves, and to deepen the experience, are the practical or experimental mystics. Some, and among them the greatest, have tried to do both. Philosophers and contemplatives alike start with the state of consciousness which arises in prayer, in communion with nature, and in love. This state of consciousness is given to us; it is a fact of experience. It is a sacred and mysterious faculty of our nature, which does not carry with it an explanation of itself, and which is evidently capable of being strengthened by cultivation, like any other faculty. To this quest some of the acutest minds and some of the noblest characters have devoted themselves. They have given up everything else, in order to find the pearl of great price. They have placed humanity heavily in their debt; they are among the greatest benefactors of mankind. Nothing can be more vulgar and shallow than to disparage the contemplative life. Journeys of discovery

B

are made no less by the philosopher or cloistered saint who "voyages through strange seas of thought alone," than by Columbus or Captain Scott, and they may be not less fruitful in results. Even the severest political economist must admit that, if the mystic produces no marketable commodities, he consumes very little of them ; and a more reasonable estimate of human costs and values will lead us to think that no labour is better expended than that which explores the way to the treasure-houses of the spirit, and shows mankind where to find those goods which are increased by being shared, and which none can take from us.

"Mysticism," says Edward Caird, "is religion in its most concentrated and exclusive form ; it is that attitude of the mind in which all other relations are swallowed up in the relation of the soul to God." This is a description of exclusive or negative mysticism, of which I shall have something to say presently : it does not cover the whole field. The mystic quest begins in every case with an inward call felt in a moment of vision. It produces a sense of dissatisfaction with ordinary experience, with those superficial aspects of life with which we are usually content. It awakens a great desire and longing to get nearer to the heart of things, and a hope that in doing so we may be rid of some of the discord and limitation and evil with which we are surrounded in this world, and which not only surround us but infect us, clogging and hampering our freedom and blinding the eyes of the soul. The discord within is even more painful than the discord without ; and we remember that at the moment of vision we seemed to have somehow escaped from it. We

escaped from it—so it seems to us when we reflect upon
what we then felt—by escaping from ourselves. We did
not feel as if our ordinary self was in communication with
the Divine Spirit, but rather as if the Divine Spirit had
for the time transformed our personality, raising it to a
higher state in which it could breathe a purer air than
that of earth, and see something of the invisible. All
forms of the mystical experience give the same impression of self-transcendence : whether we pray, or yield
ourselves to the " something more deeply interfused "
in the life of nature, or enter into that perfect sympathy
with another person when the two are " no more twain
but one," there is the same assurance that the partition-
walls of individuality have broken down, and yet that
at such moments we are more truly alive and more fully
ourselves than ever before. Thus the subject of this
experience, when he reflects on what he has seen and felt
on the holy mount, is driven to distinguish a lower from
a higher self, and to connect the disquietude of his inner
life with the lower self. He begins to think that his
happiness and salvation consist in getting rid of the lower
self altogether. All through the writings of the mystics
runs this craving to be delivered from the separated self,
and we have such utterances as this from Angelus
Silesius :—

" Nichts anders stürzet dich in Höllenschlund hinein
Als das verhasste Wort (merk's wohl !) das Mein und Dein."

Hence the severity of the purgative stage of the mystic's
discipline ; he wishes to break the bonds which confine
him to the lower life, the world of claims and counter-
claims. And hence the danger of emptying experience

in the hope of purifying it, the peril of the *via negativa* which critics have so often emphasised. But it is not fair to take this possible aberration as the essence of mysticism itself. The best mystical writings are full of warnings against the danger.

I think we may enumerate the characteristics of mystical religion as follows. (1) It is a disinterested quest of the absolutely real and good and beautiful. It is disinterested : the quest is for its own sake, never for anything outside itself. " If a man will seek the Good for anything beyond itself, he will never find it." And it is a quest of the Absolute. The mystic's goal is God Himself—the unchanging, eternal fountain of all being, the summit of all reality. There is no relativity in the mystic's philosophy, when we reach the end of it. His values are absolute ; he desires and hopes to reach the bare truth, the unconditional good, the beauty which Plato describes and contrasts with the visible beauties which we know on earth. (2) The mystic stakes all to gain all ; he gives his whole self, because if anything is kept back the quest is vain. As Manilius says :—

" Quid caelo dabimus ? Quantum est, quo veneat omne ?
Impendendus homo est, Deus esse ut possit in ipso."

Huxley once said : " It does not take much of a man to be a Christian, but it takes all there is of him." (3) He is committed to a life of strenuous labour, though the labour is mostly internal. The prize can be won only at the price of lifelong struggle. (4) Although the journey is through darkness to light, and although, as Isaac Pennington says, " All truth is shadow except the last," yet there is *immediacy* all through. Something within us is in contact with the Divine ; there is a " spark " at the core of the soul which was kindled at the altar in heaven, and which even sin cannot quite extinguish. (5) The goal is a living object of love, a God who draws souls like a magnet. (6) Beatitude is a form of enriched and enhanced life, not nothingness, whatever some mystics may say about entering into the silence, and being free from life's vain shadows. Not *nirvana*, but peace bathed in love, is his aim ; and his path is a dying life, not a living death.

The journey has been mapped out by many mystics of many creeds, countries, and centuries. The charts correspond so closely that we may be sure that those who describe the road have actually traversed it. The most philosophical scheme is that of Plotinus, the prince of intellectual mystics. For him the soul is a microcosm, which has affinities with every grade of existence, from the highest to the lowest. It may choose to live among shadows, here and hereafter ; or it may give itself to the great adventure, using the spiritual faculty " which all have, but few use." It must begin by punctually performing those social duties to which he gives the name of the political virtues ; it must next embark on the task of self-purgation, which he compares to the work of a sculptor chiselling and scraping a block of marble, till the statue imprisoned in it stands out clean and fresh ; and then, for those who are called to mount higher, comes the more glorious quest which is its own reward. For the soul may become spirit ; it may live in the world of the eternal Ideas, where distinctions remain but separation ceases. In this world, which is the fully real world,

blessed spirits " see themselves in others. For there all
things are transparent, and there is nothing dark or
opaque, but everyone is manifest to everyone internally,
and all things are manifest; for light is manifest to
light. For everyone has all things in himself, and sees
all things in others; so that all things are everywhere,
and all is all, and each is all, and infinite the glory." This
is the heaven of Plotinus. It can be our home only when
we are fit to dwell there. For we become what we see,
and we can only see what we are ready to become. We
are what we care about and think upon and love; and
the movement is *ascendere per semetipsum supra semetipsum ;* for the self and its environment are glorified
together. We may say parenthetically that, while
Platonic mysticism looks to this rich and full spiritual
world as the culminating revelation of reality—of the
world as it is in God's sight, Asiatic mysticism (and many
Europeans belong to the same type) tends to leap over
this crowning stage in the ascent, and to pass beyond
existence to the absolute One, the ineffable Absolute of
which nothing positive can be predicated. Plotinus, as
is well known, makes room in his system for the vision of
the One. As a High Priest on solemn occasions enters
into the Holy of Holies, so the soul, " possessed by intense love of him, divests herself of all form which she
has, even of that derived from spirit; she becomes
neither good nor bad nor aught else, that she may receive
him only, him alone, she alone." In this state the One
makes his presence felt, " and they are no more two but
one, and the soul is no more conscious of the body, nor
the body of the mind, but she knows that she has that

which she desired, that she is where no deception can come, and that she would not exchange her bliss for the whole heaven of heavens."

This is the mystical trance, which many prophets and wise men have desired to see, and they have sometimes seen it. In the best mystical writers it occupies less space than is usually supposed. In Neoplatonism it is, as it were, superimposed on a system which in the main is logical and rationalistic. It was, for thinkers of this school, an exceedingly rare experience, and those critics who have supposed that the aim of the whole discipline was to " swoon into the Absolute " are mistaken. In the mysticism of the cloister it fills a larger space and is regarded rather differently. " Mystical theology " came to be closely connected with strange stories of super- natural visitations, which the modern psychologist can only regard as signs of mental disturbance. The official mystical literature of the Roman Catholic Church is not very edifying reading, so much attention is paid to miraculous favours which are supposed to have been given to contemplative saints. It is true that the best guides instruct their consultants not to overvalue these experiences, and even tell them that they are frequently sent to encourage a beginner in the spiritual ascent, who finds after a time that they are withdrawn. It is clear from the evidence that these " mystical phenomena " belong to the ascetic life of the cloister. They have no place in the experience of philosopher-mystics. They are undoubtedly a genuine experience, but it is equally certain that they have no objective reality, and that they are not wholesome. Thy mystical state can be induced

by self-hypnotisation of various kinds—by long meditation concentrated upon one idea, by fasting, or by fixing
the eyes on some bright object.   It was discovered em-
pirically, long before medical psychology studied the
subject, that lasting impressions can be produced by this
method, and that the will may be strengthened—for
instance, to resist certain temptations—by this kind of
hypnotism. But undoubtedly the desire to receive super-
natural favours impelled many to submit to the discipline
which predisposes the mind to fall into this state.   Intense pleasure is often felt while the trance lasts ; but it
frequently has to be paid for by equally intense nervous
prostration, during which the patient believes himself to
have been abandoned by God, and sinks into extreme
misery and terror.   Moreover, it was admitted to be very
difficult to distinguish " divine mysticism " from " dia-
bolical imitations " ; and a strange pseudo-science came
into existence, with rules for discerning between heavenly
and infernal visitations.   All this belongs to the patho-
logy of the subject. The mystical temperament has a
strong tendency to organic enjoyment, to transferred
voluptuous feeling.   So quite unconsciously the mystical
experience has in some cases been perverted into an
obscure form of erotomania, in which the ideal object
takes the place of an earthly lover.   Christian mysticism,
however, has been almost wholly free from the really
impure perversions which are frequent in the mystical
literature of Asia. The typical mystical emotion is a
compound of awe and tenderness, and the element of awe
has protected the Christian visionaries, whose eroticism,
when present, has been unconscious, and, though doubt-

less unwholesome, has been restrained and subordinate. Modern psychology has thrown some light on these obscure mental conditions. Attention has also been given lately to the oscillations of the religious sentiment, a normal experience, but much more pronounced among the mystics, whose nervous organisation is naturally unstable and excitable, or has become so from over-stimulation. The principle of alternation seems to be a law of all life, and in religious feeling too, day and night, summer and winter, follow each other. It has been said that " God is sometimes given to us as *absent*." Thus the rapturous ecstasy and the dark night of the soul are only the most violent manifestations of a tendency to alternate warmth and coldness in devotion which appears to be normal : the knowledge that it is so may comfort some who find these oscillations unaccountable and distressing.

But though the psychological study of mystical pheno-mena has thrown much light on the physical and psy-chical concomitants of mystical states, I do not think that it has been altogether an advantage for the under-standing of mysticism. The numerous books, chiefly French and American, which have investigated mys-ticism from this side, have failed completely to enter into the mind of the mystic himself. For psychology is the science which studies states of consciousness as such ; it is not concerned with the objective reality or the value of the revelations which are so communicated. But the mystic cares nothing about his states of consciousness ; he is willing to say with St. Paul, " Whether I was in the body or out of the body I cannot tell ; God knoweth."

For him the sole question of importance is whether he has been in contact with a higher reality than in his ordinary consciousness, or not.   It is impossible to enter into his state of mind by compiling tables of statistics and issuing questionnaires.   The psychologist also tends to give too much attention to the abnormal and unhealthy ;   he often treats mysticism as a type of mental aberration, instead of, as it is, an outgrowth, sometimes an overgrowth, of a faculty which is extremely common and perfectly wholesome.   Some of the American school, it is true, have not fallen into this error.   Questions have been put to a large number of persons as to whether they have had any experience of conscious communion with God, in such a sense that they could base their belief in God upon it.   In answering one questioner, only twenty-one out of seventy-seven did not reply in the affirmative. It is quite possible that the decay of authority in religion has driven most people to pay more regard to the testimony of the inner light, and that in consequence the proportion of those whose faith rests on what it has become the fashion to call religious experience is greater now than at other times.   But who that has formed the habit of private prayer could fail to answer " yes " to the inquiry mentioned above ?

The question that may legitimately be asked is not as to the reality of the mystical experience, but as to its rank and value.   And here we must distinguish. Sometimes the consciousness of communion with God is a calm and gentle feeling, compounded, as I have said, of awe and love, a feeling which opens new vistas to the eye of the soul, but does not banish reason from her seat.

But the literature of mysticism tells of other phenomena —of trances passing sometimes into catalepsy; of wild excitement finding a vent in shouts and maniacal dances; of hallucinations of sight, hearing, and smell. Now, if we take the life of Christ as our example, we shall infer that religion should never be a mood of excitement. Our Lord spent whole nights in prayer, but there is not a trace in the Gospels of rapturous ecstasy or strange visions. "Let not your heart be troubled," is His parting message to His disciples. It is in St. Paul, not in the Master Himself, that we find an example of "mystical phenomena." And St. Paul speaks of these "visions and revelations" as a rare thing in his experience, as they were in that of Plotinus. Nevertheless, he valued them, and believed that once at least, "fourteen years ago," he had been caught up into the third heaven. Nor do I see any reason to doubt that spiritual knowledge is sometimes communicated in a vision. We need have no theory about what actually happens in the mind. When we are dealing with purely internal states, the difference between subjective and objective has no meaning. The mystic says, " I, yet not I, but Christ in me," or, " The Spirit itself beareth witness with our spirit," and " maketh intercession for us with groanings unutterable." It is part of the philosophy of mysticism that personality is no hard and fast thing, but that in passing into the realm of spirit we experience the divine no longer as an object but as an atmosphere, the source and sustenance of our new life.

We cannot determine the proper place of the mystical experience, because it is no fixed, self-identical thing. It is an "untravelled world, whose margin fades for ever and for ever as we move." As that which was once in a luminous haze comes into clear daylight, a fresh vision of cloud-capped towers and gorgeous palaces floats dimly into view. There is no rest, no sitting still, no time for voluptuous dreaming, in the spiritual journey, until we reach the land which is still very far off, though it lies all about us and within us, closer than breathing and nearer than hands and feet. We do not ask to see the distant scene ; we know that we must climb by degrees. "Beloved, now are we the sons of God ; and it doth not yet appear what we shall be ; but we know that when He shall be manifested, we shall be like Him, for we shall see Him as He is." The last words express the fundamental faith of all mystics, that like is known by like, and only by like. "We could not see the sun"—so they tell us in an illustration which is a favourite with them—"if we had not something sun-like in our eyes."

It is often said that the mystic's experiences are of no value except to himself. They may be good evidence to himself, but from their nature they are not transferable. But there does not seem to be any reason why the testimony of the mystics should be less trustworthy than that of other specialists. Their reports show a remarkable unanimity ; it is impossible to guess the date or nationality of a mystical work ; we often cannot even tell whether a quotation comes from a Christian, a Mohammedan Sufi, or a Buddhist. Those who have taken the same path seem, as might be expected if the journey is a real one, to see the same things. Of course, if we choose to believe that we are cut off from any knowledge of things as they are, or if we believe that there is no such thing as absolute reality and absolute truth, we shall not attach much value to the visions of men and women whose lives have been one continuous quest of the absolutely true and good ; but in that case, it seems to me, we have given up theism altogether. If there is a God, and if God is knowable, the testimony of those who declare that they have found Him, or that He has found them, is worthy of respect.

And yet there is this great difficulty, that the vision cannot be described. All the mystics have admitted as much. To give one instance where it would be easy to find twenty, Angela of Foligno, while dictating her revelations to her amanuensis, would frequently exclaim, " I blaspheme, brother, I blaspheme ! All that I have said is nothing, and there is nothing that I can say." Myers makes St. Paul exclaim :—

> " O could I tell, ye surely would believe it,
> O could I only say what I have seen !
> How should I tell, or how can ye receive it,
> How, till He bringeth you where I have been ! "

FitzGerald, in his *Attar*, describes how the moths sent messengers to find their idol the flame. The first and second come back with slight and uncertain intelligence. A third goes in their place,

> " who, spurred with true desire,
> Plunging at once into the sacred fire,
> Folded his wings within, till he became
> One colour and one substance with the flame.
> He only knew the flame who in it burned,
> And only he could tell who ne'er to tell returned."

It is notoriously difficult, or even impossible, to describe a sunset from memory. And the mystical vision is concerned with things more impalpable than a sunset, things which language was not framed to describe; it is sometimes faint and always fugitive; and it is generally —so at least Plotinus found, and gives us his explanation —formless. It is not like anything else, and so cannot be visualised, or imparted to others by the use of images. Those who have had these experiences long to remember them, and long to impart them. But then they must trust to their memory; in other words, they must try to be outside and inside the mystical state at the same time. The intellect is set to work, and begins to schematise and set in order a vision which had no form and no parts. If they try to recall the states of mind which led up to the vision, they will probably narrate an orderly progression of which they were not conscious at the time. Doubts, hesitations, and reactions are forgotten. And often their narratives are unconsciously influenced by suggestion from outside; they have talked to directors, or they have read books. As a rule, the mystics have written their autobiographies when they were far advanced in their progress; their books are souvenirs and memoirs rather than journals. Teresa wrote her life in 1562 and 1566; but her " mystical period " began in 1555. The same may be said of Julian of Norwich, of Suso, and of Madame Guyon. No doubt all were perfectly honest; but we can judge how treacherous the memory of psychical states is when we compare Augustine's account of his conversion, written many years after, in his *Confessions*, with the short and little-known treatises which he wrote at the time.

There is, therefore, no substitute for first-hand experience in the spiritual life. We must believe the explorers of the high places of the unseen world when they tell us that they have been there, and found what they sought. But they cannot really tell us *what* they found ; if we wish to see what they have seen, we must live as they have lived. This is not possible for all, or nearly all. There is such a thing as genius in the religious life, and genius is rare. There are also unmystical types of religion ; there are good men and women who live ever " in their great Taskmaster's eye," and whose religion is a matter of duty and obedience, rather than of love and communing with God. It would be a great mistake to rank these below the more intuitive and contemplative type, which may sometimes be associated with a weaker will and a less robust conscience. For the danger of antinomianism is never far off from the mystic ; where the inner life is so much more important than the outer, there may be a temptation either to inactivity or to unscrupulousness in action. The discipline of Catholicism has restrained many who might otherwise have broken loose morally, as some of the heretical mystics did, or were accused by their enemies of doing. But the lives of the greater mystics will bear the most rigorous inspection ; and we may surely say that it is to a large extent through such men and women that the Spirit of God kindles the fire of divine love and the longing for divine knowledge in the hearts of others. Nor should anyone acquiesce in being without this precious gift until he has striven long and patiently to acquire it. The practice of the presence of God may involve very many hours of hard work ; but the reward is great ; for this is the joy that no man can take from us ; this is the faith which is the human side of divine grace, an experiment which is becoming an experience, a foretaste and assurance of the rest that remaineth for the people of God.

CHAPTER II

THE SOUL'S THIRST

THE idea of thirst has no terrors for us in this country. Hunger is unhappily not unknown to the very poor; but the " cup of cold water " can always be had for the asking. But in the parched-up land of Palestine, surrounded by waterless deserts—a country where even the rivers are swallowed up in the sands or dried by the fierce sun, so that they never reach the sea, it is very different. The misery of thirst, one of the greatest torments that the human frame can endure, was a familiar thing to the Jews, as it is to those who inhabit the interior of Australia. I have heard of a young Englishman out there, who lost his way in the bush, and wandered up and down, and round and round, till his body, contorted with his last agony, was found within a mile of the spring which he was vainly seeking. The word thirst, in such climates, calls up the idea of the most passionate and painful craving that a man can experience. It is the agonised protest of the body against being deprived of its most vital need. If not assuaged, it is the prelude to the most dreadful of deaths.

When we remember this, we shall realise the full meaning of those passages in the Bible where thirst is

C

used metaphorically. " Like as the hart desireth the water-brooks, so longeth my soul after thee, O God. My soul is athirst for God, yea even for the living God." " O God, thou art my God, early will I seek thee. My soul thirsteth for thee, my flesh also longeth after thee, in a barren and dry land where no water is." " Ho every one that thirsteth, come ye to the waters." And in our Blessed Lord's own words, " Blessed are they that hunger and thirst after righteousness, for they shall be filled." Or again, in that wonderful discourse with the woman of Samaria by Jacob's well, you re-member how our Lord tells the woman about the " living water " which He can give to those who ask for it. " Whosoever drinketh of this water [from the well] shall thirst again ; but whosoever drinketh of the water that I shall give him shall never thirst : but the water that I shall give him shall be in him a well of water, springing up into everlasting life." The doctrine of Christ as the living water runs through these early chapters of St. John, recurring, like a musical phrase, in hints and symbolic language—the water that was made wine, in chapter ii, the water of the new birth in iii, the living water in iv, the cleansing water of Bethesda in v, the miracle of Gennasaret in vi, and then in vii the declara-tion that makes all clear : " On the last day, the great day of the feast, Jesus stood and cried, If any man thirst let him come unto me and drink. He that believeth on me, out of his belly shall flow rivers of living water." It is for Christ himself that the parched soul is athirst ; He is (as St. Augustine says in his commentary on the Sermon on the Mount) our righteousness ; it is with him

that they are filled who hunger and thirst after righteousness.   At the very end of the Bible, in the last chapter of
Revelation, we have an echo of Isaiah's words.   " The
Spirit and the Bride say Come.   And let him that is
athirst come.   And whosoever will, let him drink of the
water of life freely."   Blessed is he that so thirsteth, for
he shall be filled.

Now let me show you a contrast.   Next to Christianity,
the noblest religion in the world is that of Buddha, the
Indian prophet and teacher who lived 500 years before
Christ.   His religion has been corrupted, as Christianity
has too often been ;   but as it came from his lips it was
pure and beautiful.   And what does Buddha say about
thirst ?   " Whom thirst conquers, thirst the contemptible, for him will suffering grow as the grass grows.
Who conquers thirst, the contemptible, which is hard
to escape in the world, from him will suffering fall away
like the water-drop from the lotus flower."   Thirst
means the passionate craving for something that we
have not got.   This, says Buddha, is the source of all
our unhappiness.   It can never be satisfied ;   for since
this world is a vain show and no real thing, all that we
try to grasp slips through our fingers, and in our attempts
to slake our thirst we fare no better than the women
in the Greek fable, who were condemned for ever to
carry water in a sieve.   Therefore, says the Indian
sage, crave for nothing, grasp at nothing.   Blessed is
he that thirsteth for nothing, for he shall be at peace.

You see here the difference between Buddhism and
Christianity.   Buddha says, Desire nothing, and then
you will not be disappointed :   turn away from earth's

vain shadows ; sink your own personality altogether, and win the untroubled rest of a dreamless sleep in the bosom of the Eternal. Christ says, You are right to thirst ; thirst is a blessed thing ; that pain and longing which you feel, you ought to feel. You must not shirk it, or try to deaden it. It is a right and natural craving, which has its right and natural satis-faction. Only, do not make a mistake as to what it is that your soul thirsts for, and where its thirst may be assuaged. " My people have committed two evils," says the Lord through the mouth of Jeremiah ; " they have forsaken me, the fountain of living waters, and have hewed them out cisterns, broken cisterns, that can hold no water." That is what men are always doing. They have not learnt the truth of St. Augus-tine's wonderful words, " Thou hast made us for thyself ; and our hearts are restless, until they rest in thee."

Alas for the portentous amount of labour that is spent upon those broken cisterns—all the great things that men attempt when they organise themselves apart from God. And then they leak ; they will not hold water ; no, not enough to slake our thirst. But they who hunger and thirst after righteousness shall be filled. Observe that our Lord makes righteousness an end in itself. It is itself that which satisfies the cravings of the soul. His beatitudes are thus very different from those of the Old Testament. The reward of obedience in Deuteronomy is, " Blessed shalt thou be in the city, and blessed shalt thou be in the field. Blessed shall be the fruit of thy body and the fruit of thy ground. Blessed shall be thy basket and thy store. The Lord shall command a blessing upon thee in thy storehouses and in all that thou settest thine hand to." Obedience, you see, is a means to an end, and the end is worldly prosperity and domestic happiness. But with Christ the reward is nothing external. He simply says, I have come to teach you what it is that can alone make a human soul blessed. Desire it earnestly and you shall have it. " Blessed are they whose soul melteth away for the very fervent desire that they have for God and his righteousness. For they shall be filled ; they shall see God ; they shall be called the children of God."

The soul of man, when it is healthy, is athirst for God ; and God only, through Christ, can slake the soul's thirst. Longing for God, for the eternally good and true and lovely, is natural to man ; it is man's most divine endowment. The thirst, as well as the living water, is the gift of God. As Christ is both Priest and Victim, so He gives both the thirst and the life-giving draught. The soul of man, when it is healthy, is athirst for God. To know that this is so, is the foundation of all true religion. This is what Christ always assumed in His teaching. Man wants to find his way to God. That is why we come to Church ; that is why we pray. And our Saviour cries to us with a loud voice, as He did on the great day of the feast, " If any man thirst, let him come unto me and drink."

Why is it that we habitually allow our religion to be pitched on a much lower key than this ? What has made our Christianity so *secular*, so unlike the original Gospel ? Are we clergy afraid, or ashamed, to appeal to that divine spark which burns and glows in the

depths of every human soul ? Do we fear that such
an appeal will awake no response, and is this why we
preach about politics, work and wages, last week's
newspapers, anything rather than the Gospel of Christ ?
The great religious teachers, who have a real message,
never lower themselves like this, and they do touch
the hearts of their hearers.

But some of you may be saying : " Alas, I do not
feel thirsty : those verses from the Psalms which you
quoted are not real to me. I never feel like that."
We none of us feel like that nearly as much as we ought.
But most assuredly if we have not that desire for God
and the spiritual world where God dwells, if we have
no hunger and thirst after that righteousness which
is Christ, we are not Christians, nor religious people
at all. How can we have that which we do not desire ?
How can we see God if we do not long to see Him ?
Do not suppose that church-going and almsgiving and
frequent communions and philanthropy are what religion
consists in. Religion is the thirst for God, and its
satisfaction.

In one of the recently discovered Sayings of Jesus
(found in the sands of Egypt) we read : " Jesus said,
I stood in the midst of the world and in the flesh I was
seen of them ; and I found all men drunken, and none
found I athirst among them, and my soul grieveth
over the sons of men, because they are blind in their
heart and see not." I found all men drunken, and
none athirst. What is the meaning of this ? Does
it mean that we have drugged ourselves with poison,
and no longer desire the living water ? Let us hope

that it is not so bad as that. Let us hope that we are only asleep and dreaming, or occupied with the unchildlike childish play which we call our work and amusement. If so, it is high time to awake out of sleep. You have not yet lost the wholesome appetite which makes the soul cry, " My soul is athirst for God ; when shall I come to appear before the presence of God ? " Recollect ; think ; pray ; do not always be in such a hurry. You know well, when you do stop to think seriously, that you are not satisfied. There is something wanting. You have been thirsty, without knowing it. Well, that thirst is the craving which God has put into you, because He wishes to satisfy it with Himself. Blessed are they that thirst, and woe to them who can thirst no longer because they are drunken with that which cannot satisfy them. " Wherefore," says Isaiah, " do ye spend your money on that which is not bread, and your labour on that which satisfieth not ? Come to the waters ; yea, come, buy wine and milk without money and without price."

It is the old, old appeal, which is out of fashion, I suppose, with many of our modern teachers. But it is what we most need to hear, now as always. " Ye are as holy as ye truly wish to be holy," said one of the old mystics. And if in response to our prayer for the living water there comes the grave question, " Can ye drink of the cup that I shall drink of ? " it is faith and love, not presumption, that answers humbly, " We are able."

" There is a cup in the hand of the Lord, and the wine is red. It is full mixed, and he poureth out of the same." Yes, the cup of suffering, and the cup of blessing, the cup of communion, are they not the same cup? Shall we, in the bitterness of our suffering, say, "Thou hast showed thy people heavy things, thou hast given us a drink of deadly wine"? Or shall we not rather find a meaning in those difficult words of St. John, "There are three that bear witness on earth, the spirit, the water, and the blood, and these three agree in one"?

CHAPTER III

THE writer of the Epistle to the Hebrews has done for
Faith what St. Paul, in I Cor. xiii, has done for Love.
He has not only given us a magnificent hymn in honour
of Faith ; he has laid down, for all time, the essentials
of Christian Faith ; he has shown us the roots of it
and the fruits of it, how it begins and where it ends.

The famous definition at the beginning of the Eleventh
Chapter is unfortunately obscure ; scholars differ as
to the meaning of an important word. The Revised
Version gives : " Now faith is the assurance [or, the
giving substance to] things hoped for, the proving [or,
test] of things not seen." The word *hypostasis* has
the meaning of substance, or reality, in the third verse
of the First Chapter ; and all through the Epistle the
distinction between heaven and earth, between spirit
and flesh, is conceived as that between substance and
shadow, truth and appearance, pattern and copy. St.
Chrysostom's note is : " For whereas things that are
matters of hope seem to be unsubstantial, Faith gives
them substance ; or rather does not give it but is itself
their being. For instance, the resurrection has not
taken place, and is not in substance, but Faith gives
it substance in our soul." St. Chrysostom means that
Faith lifts us out of the time series, in which the past
has ceased to be and the future is not yet, and exalts

us into the eternal world, in which the future is as real as the present. In the Ninth Chapter we read that Christ offered Himself to God "through an eternal Spirit"—in the world of timeless reality. The two most sympathetic of modern commentators on the Epistle, Bishop Westcott and Dr. DuBose, are unwilling to give up the rendering "substance." Westcott paraphrases Chrysostom's note in his own words. DuBose says: "Beneath or behind the things that are seen and are temporal there is an Eternal Unseen. What is it? The Word of God. If this answer is not true, there is no object or function of Faith, and no religion. Faith is not only assurance; it is the present possession, the very substance and reality of its object. Assurance is substance, Faith is Fact, promise is fulfilment, hope is possession and fruition, because Faith is the laying hold of and uniting itself with that Word of God which is at once the substance of all reality and the light of all truth."

On the other hand it may be objected that if Faith is identified with substance, its objects are reduced to subjective illusion, and also that it is doubtful whether "that which *gives* substance to" can be got out of the Greek word. For this reason, most scholars prefer "assurance"; though Faith is certainly not *mere* "assurance" (*fiducia*) as Luther seems to have taught, and though "that which gives substance to" is the teaching of the Epistle about Faith.

Perhaps the Egyptian papyri have thrown a new light on this difficult word. Dr. Milligan finds that *hypostasis* is a legal term used to denote the collection of papers bearing upon the possession of a piece of property, the title-deeds, as we should say. If this is the meaning here, the writer of the Epistle defines Faith neither as the substance of things hoped for, nor as assurance of their existence, but as a kind of pledge which gives us the right to claim them. The second disputed word, *elenchos*, " proving," would fit in very well with this explanation, which is in any case highly interesting.

There are two other notable sayings about Faith in this Epistle, which we ought not to neglect. One is in this Chapter. " He that cometh to God must believe that He is, and that He is the Rewarder of them that diligently seek him." The other is in Chapter Five. " Faith is seeing the invisible One," that is, God. Faith is seeing God during our earthly pilgrimage. St. Augustine's comment on this is : " They were still wandering and seeking their country. But with Christ as their leader they could not go astray. Their journey was the vision of God." That is enough for this latter passage. The other, " he that cometh to God," etc., needs a little more thought. The words are as profound as they are simple. They raise the greatest of all problems : Is the source of goodness and moral value the same as the source of the reality that we know ? Is the God of nature the same as the God of religion ? The eminent Danish philosopher, Höffding, who is not thinking of our Epistle at all, says, " It is only by an act of Faith that a harmony is supposed between the series of value and of cause." That is to say, there are two things which we must believe about God, if

we wish to believe rightly about Him. The first is
that He actually exists, objectively and eternally, now
and always. The second is, that the moral law is also
a fact—that our trust in the final victory of right over
wrong is sanctioned by the deepest laws of the universe.
And we can only believe these two things, which are
the two sides of the same coin (we cannot have one
without the other, since the idea of God requires them
both), we can only believe these two things by Faith.
Faith asserts that God is, and that He is the Rewarder
of them that diligently seek him. God, who is the
source of all reality, is also the source of our sense of
right and wrong : and He is on the side of the right.
God is not fighting for His own existence ; He *is*, the
supreme and eternal fact. And in spite of all
appearances to the contrary, He governs as well as
reigns. As Julian of Norwich says, " In my folly I often
wondered why the beginning of sin was not letted ; but
Jesus in this vision answered and said, Sin is behovable,
but all shall be well, and all shall be well, and all manner
of thing shall be well."

How do we know this ? Do we simply say it to keep
up our spirits ? I do not think that many of us would
care to live on blind hopes and vain imaginings. Or do
we know it as a matter of immediate intuition ? Are
we to say, " I know because I know, and I cannot argue
about it " ? Some have used this argument, perhaps
rather too conscious that you cannot refute a man who
tells you that he has private and authentic information
that what he says is true. But it is not sound. Not
that I have any doubt whatever that this immediate

experience of God's presence is possible. Many have
had it ; many have it now.   But surely it is the privilege
reserved for those who have striven for it as the ambitious
man strives for wealth or power.   It is not and cannot
be the foundation of Faith.   It is the crown of that
divine love in which Faith finds its fulfilment, its justification, and its reward.   We cannot see God until
the image of God in which we were made has been
converted by a life of service and devotion into a likeness
of God stamped upon our souls.   Until we are like Him,
we cannot see Him as He is.   Most of us have had
glimpses in prayer of what this vision may be.   But
these experiences are so fugitive, and above all so formless, that we cannot afterwards picture them to ourselves,
much less explain them to others.   And they answer
no particular questions ;   they add nothing to our
knowledge—nothing definite and tangible.   When we
approach the great problems with only these fitful gleams
to guide us, we understand why this Epistle insists that
the religious life must begin with Faith.   Faith is an
act of self-consecration, in which the will, the intellect,
and the affections all have their place.   It is the resolve
to live as if certain things were true, in the confident
assurance that they are true, and that we shall one day
find out for ourselves that they are true.   The process
of verification begins as soon as we have honestly set
out to climb.   We ourselves change, and the world
changes to our sight.   The landscape opens out more
and more as we get further up the hill.

Faith is a kind of climbing instinct, which draws us
upward and onward.   It is at first quite vague and

undifferentiated, and partly subconscious. Then it takes
shape as a homage to, and craving after, God, who shines
as a triple constellation in the spiritual firmament, as the
Source of the Good, the True, and the Beautiful. The
God of Faith is revealed to us under these three attributes.
As parts of God's nature they are eternal facts.
Whatever is real and permanent in the world that we
know, partakes in these qualities. The triple star shines
ever above us, with light blended yet distinct. It shines
above us, and it shines within us, too. The inner light
is the light of Faith, and the outer light is the light of
Grace ; and these two are only the two sides—the
human and the divine aspects—of the same illumination.
It comes from God ; but it does not come—it could not
come—into us from outside. It is the Spirit of God
within us that discerns and bears witness to the Spirit
of God outside us.

This is the heart of Faith ; this is the one primary
ground of Faith. It is a light which lighteth every
man—every man worthy of the name. Certainly nothing great or good is ever done without it.

And let us note this—for it is very important. The
normal movement of Faith is double, like the action
of the valves of the heart. Our whole nature is ennobled
and enhanced as we try to follow the gleam, dimly
perceived perhaps, but deeply believed in. And this
enrichment takes the double form of expansion and
concentration. Let us never forget that one is as
necessary as the other. If we read the writings of the
mystics, we shall find that nearly all the stress is laid
on concentration. We are to draw all things into one,

detaching ourselves from whatever we cannot translate into a symbol of the divine. " Go not forth," they say to us ; " return into thyself ; in the inner man is the habitation of truth." This is indeed a lesson that we have to learn. The inner chamber must be made pure for the divine Guest. We are not to be careful and troubled about many things, when one thing is needful. Prayer and meditation will teach us much that we cannot learn in any other way. If we cannot find God, it is perhaps because He is at home, while we are abroad ; He is ready for us, while we are too busy to attend to Him.

Yes, this is half the truth, but only half. In Jacob's vision, referred to, you will remember, by our Lord in St. John, the angels were not only climbing up the ladder, they were also coming down it.

What does this mean ? It means that we are not to run away from life even to find God, but that we are to come back with our treasure as soon as we have found it. Have we succeeded in finding God in the world ? Then let us try to find the world in God. Let us try to make all things according to the pattern showed us in the mount.

This is, I am sure, the right way to look at the rival claims of action and devotion. Both are necessary ; no spiritual act is complete till it has been first prayed and then done. And after that comes the call to a purer prayer and a nobler act. Such is the spiral stair by which man may ascend to heaven.

It seems to me that this is the deepest truth about sacraments. The particular sacraments are meant to

teach us that all life is sacramental. Every deliberate
act should be, in a sense, the outward sign of inward
grace. A sacrament is more than a symbol. A symbol
leads us from the lower to the higher; a sacrament
brings us back again to earth, but infuses a heavenly
meaning and divine potency into common things and
actions.

Such, then, is Faith in its essence—it is the human
aspect of divine Grace. This alone is primary. All
else, creeds, dogmas, philosophies, moralities, ritual and
cultus, are secondary. It is right and natural that
our faith should create these forms; most of us cannot
do without them. But they are all Faith's instruments;
they are not the foundation on which Faith is built.

And yet we hear some superior young man talking
as if only doubts about miracles prevented him from
being a St. Francis!

The Epistle makes it clear that Faith is from first to
last an *activity* of the soul. It is not a passive acceptance
of dogmas or of a scheme of salvation. Hartley Coleridge
has an admirable stanza about this:—

> " Think not the faith by which the just shall live
>   Is a dead creed, a map correct of heaven,
>   Far less a feeling fond and fugitive,
>   A thoughtless gift, withdrawn as soon as given,
>   It is an affirmation and an act
>   Which makes eternal truth be present fact."

This is exactly the meaning of the famous definition in
Hebrews xi. But it is a formidable task to " make
eternal truth be present fact " ! It is easy for philosophers to talk about, but it means translating spiritual

into temporal values without loss, and how can we do this ? The forms of Faith are not Faith itself, and there is nothing infallible about them. Thy must change. The hopes, too, to which our Faith gives substance, may have to undergo great changes. This is the lesson which the writer draws from the roll-call of the Old Testament heroes.

The roll of honour is almost entirely of men of *action*, not of saints and prophets. He names the men who legislated and fought for Israel, her great patriots. And then he passes to the martyrs for their country—those who " were stoned, were sawn asunder, slain with the sword, who wandered about in sheepskins and goatskins, in deserts and caves of the earth." Those of whom the world was not worthy were fugitives and vagabonds on the earth ! And all alike, heroes and martyrs, having had a witness borne to them through their Faith, received *not* the promise. None of them ! Nor was the promise ever fulfilled as they had pictured to themselves. God had provided some better thing, which He gave them instead. That, I think we may dare to say, is God's way. How seldom does the great man achieve what he meant to do ! Whether he wants to liberate his country, to reform its constitution or its religion—whatever he has pinned his life's hope on —he generally achieves not this but something else. And are we to suppose that the great cloud of witnesses now complain ? No. They do not say, " We have laboured in vain, we have spent our strength for nought and in vain." Hope has died to live, but Faith has not been deceived or finally disappointed.

D

And we too, in our hope for ourselves, our families, and our dear country, must be content to commit ourselves into God's hands in Faith. The future is hidden from us, mercifully perhaps. It may not bring what we most wish for. Our hopes may have to be transmuted like the Messianic hopes of the first Christians.

We believe that God is, and that He is the rewarder of them that diligently seek Him. What that reward will be, here and hereafter, we know not. Here it may be the privilege of suffering. It is the trials of Faith, its pains and disappointments, that are the sources of its real triumph, " the victory that overcometh the world." In the other world, too, there will be great surprises for us. But when, by God's grace, we hear the words, " Enter thou into the joy of thy Lord," we shall have the fruit of our Faith and Hope, which is to pass into Love. This is the teaching of Clement of Alexandria, than whom no one has written more beautifully about Faith. " Faith," he says, " which the heathen describe as futile and barbarous, is a voluntary anticipation, the assent of piety, the assurance of things hoped for, the evidence of things not seen, as the inspired Apostle says. There is a first kind of saving change from heathenism to Faith, a second from Faith to Knowledge ; and Knowledge, as it passes on into Love, begins at once to establish a mutual friendship between the knower and the known. Perhaps he who has reached this stage is ' equal to the angels.' "

CHAPTER IV

HOPE

LIKE all other Christian virtues and graces, Hope has a deep foundation. It is part of a quite distinctive view of life, which belongs to Christianity, and was brought into the world, as a new revelation, by Jesus Christ. If we want to know what fresh ideas and new convictions the Gospel introduced, we cannot do better than study carefully the new words which the first Christians were obliged to use. We find in the New Testament a whole list of moral virtues which had no place, or a different place, in non-Christian writings. Such words are love, joy, peace, faith, hope, and humility. When Christianity was fresh from the mint it needed all these words. They belong to Christianity, and are characteristic of it, as " liberty, equality, and fraternity " belonged to the French Revolution, or as " justice, temperance, prudence, and fortitude " belonged to Pagan ethics. It is well worth while to collect all that is said in the New Testament about each of these new virtues, and to think out for ourselves what they mean and how they are related to each other. If we can understand what these words meant to the early Christians, we shall know what Christianity stood for, and still stands for, in the world.

No one before Christ had made Hope a moral virtue.
To the Pagans it was a gift of doubtful value, an illusion
which helps us to endure life, and a valuable spur to
action; but, on the whole, an *ignis fatuus.* Very
characteristic is the Greek epitaph which that modern
Pagan, Lord Brougham, inscribed on his villa at Cannes :

> " I've entered port. Fortune and Hope, adieu !
> Make game of others, for I've done with you."

Hope, for Pagan philosophy, as for Schopenhauer, is
the bait by which Nature gets her hook in our nose and
induces us to serve her purposes, which are not ours.

Now turn to the New Testament. It must be an
accident, though a strange one, that the word Hope
does not occur in the four Gospels. There is plenty
of the *thing* in our Lord's teaching, but for the name
we must turn to the Epistles. St. Paul emphasises
very strongly the central position which Hope holds in
the Christian character.   His three cardinal virtues
are Faith, Hope, and Love, an entirely original triad
which was afterwards adopted by the Neoplatonists,
who added Truth as a fourth. It is very significant
that St. Paul condemns Paganism partly on the ground
that its adherents " have no Hope, and are without
God in the world." He adds that they are " hateful
and hating one another." Want of Faith, want of
Hope, and want of Love—these are the three defects
which made Pagan life, as he saw it, miserable.
Christians, he says, are saved by Hope. Christ is
Himself our Hope ; Christ in us is the Hope of glory.
Three times he couples Hope with patience ; " remem-
bering your patience of Hope in Jesus " ; " patience

worketh experience, and experience Hope "; " through
patience and comfort of the Scriptures we have Hope."
Equally instructive is the Epistle to the Hebrews,
which is a treatise upon Hope no less than upon Faith.
Hope is an anchor of the soul, sure and steadfast.
It is Faith directed towards the future, Faith in God's
promises, which nevertheless are often not fulfilled
as we desire and expect. The whole history of the
chosen people shows how Hope must often die to live ;
how it must often surrender its fairest dreams, springing
again after bitter disappointment ; for so is the will of
God, who " provides some better thing," something
which one day, though not now, we shall know to be
better than what we hoped for. For no pure Hope
shall ever wither, except that a purer may grow out of
its roots. In the First Epistle of St. Peter we read
that we have been begotten again unto a living Hope
by the resurrection of Jesus Christ from the dead ;
and in the First Epistle of St. John the content of
Christian Hope is set forth with perfect clearness.
" Beloved, now are we children of God, and it is not yet
made manifest what we shall be. We know that if
He shall be manifested, we shall be like Him ; for we
shall see Him even as He is. And every one that hath
this Hope set on Him purifieth himself even as He is
pure."

Now what is this Hope ? What is the Hope that is
a sister-virtue of Faith and Love ? Is it merely a
temper of hopefulness ? Is it merely the habit, or the
faculty, of looking at the bright side of things ? We all
know the value of hopefulness. The proverbs of many

nations emphasise it. " He that regardeth the clouds shall not reap." " Lose heart, lose all." There are many other sayings to the same effect. In medical practice the importance of encouraging the patient is well known. Hopefulness means happiness, and happiness tends to health and efficiency. Is this the Christian secret ?

No, it is not. Christianity does not bid us play tricks with our souls in order to produce any results, external or internal. Christianity does not wish us to believe anything except because it is true. And when Christianity says that a thing is true, it does not mean merely that it works, nor that we should be happier and better for believing it. It means that what it tells us to believe is objectively true, part of the constitution of the world in which we live, part of the laws of God's creation. It may be helpful here to give two or three quotations from great theologians, who have analysed the contents of Christian Hope. " Hope," says St. Thomas Aquinas, " is a divinely infused quality of the soul, whereby with certain trust we expect those good things of the life eternal which are to be attained by the grace of God." " True wisdom," says Dorner, " is the same as Christian Hope, which is neither ignorance concerning the future, nor uncertainty and mere empty desire, but is the principle of that true Christian view of the world which is quickened by love into fruitful activity." Bishop Francis Paget says : " If we are hopeful, in the Christian sense of the word, we shall live and think and work with the resolute conviction that the goal and aim of human life, for ourselves and for others, is that which the Bible declares it to be. How high it is, how surpassing in glory, we may but partly see. To be conformed to the Son of God, to be like Him, seeing Him as He is ; to be pure even as He is pure ; to be without stain, without sin, without temptation ; to live wholly in the peace and joy and love of God and of those who are like Him, and so to live for ever—these are thoughts which we but faintly and slowly realise ; which it is very hard to associate with what we know of ourselves now. But they are plainly and repeatedly set forth in the Bible as the divinely intended issue and fulfilment of a human life ; as that which we should bear in mind when we are thinking what men are meant for, and what is, and is not, worth taking trouble about."*

Christian hopefulness, then, is the temper natural to immortal spirits under temporal probation, who know that their heavenly Father loves them, that their Lord has redeemed them, and that the Holy Spirit is ever with them to help their infirmities.

But our generation is not satisfied with this answer. " We know (they say) that this is the Christian doctrine, and a very comforting doctrine it is. But meanwhile we have to live in this world. We are deeply interested in this world, and we think we are right to be interested in the present and future of humanity, especially in a time like this, when European civilisation, with all its hardly earned gains, seems to be in danger. Is Christianity optimistic about this world, or only about that other world which we cannot see, the land that is very far off ?" We must face this question quite squarely, for it is the

* *Hallowing of Work*, pp. 36, 37.

question which is in all men's minds to-day. I do not
say that we ought to approve of the temper in which it
is usually put. Our religion has been grievously secular-
ised during a long period of unexampled security and
gross material prosperity. But the longing to improve
our civilisation and to advance the kingdom of God upon
earth has taken a strong hold upon the noblest spirits
of our time, and surely we cannot wish it otherwise.
Our message cannot and must not be that these hopes
and ambitions are to be abandoned. We are not to
cry : " O that I had wings as a dove, for then would I
flee away and be at rest." That cry of world-weariness
now sounds like selfishness, almost like treason. This
world is but a shadow of heaven ; but, as Isaac Pennington says, " the shadow is a true shadow, as the
substance is a true substance." If we give up trying
to find the hand of God in human history, while we
fix our eyes only on eternity, our minds will dwell
in an empty heaven ; we shall grasp at infinity and
find only zero.

The Old Testament will be our best guide, if we treat
it as the record of an education lasting through many
centuries. God was training the Jewish people for the
glorious destiny which He had prepared for them " in
the fulness of time." Now Judaism, unlike Paganism,
was always a religion of Hope. The Jews believed that
God is revealed in history, that (as a German proverb
says) " the history of the world is the judgment of the
world." They believed that God rewards righteousness
and punishes iniquity ; that His judgments are executed
in this life, though sometimes slowly ; and that He will

not suffer the righteous to fall for ever. This is why, for the Jews, insight always takes the form of foresight; this is why their preachers of righteousness were always prophets.

The main subject of the Old Testament is the conflict of this faith with the hard facts of life. The Jews, as St. Paul most truly says, " against Hope believed in Hope." They would not abandon their hopefulness and trust in God, though no nation ever suffered such cruel disappointments. And it is strange how very slow they were to give up their belief that, somehow or other, justice is done openly and in this life. It is easy to blame them for this; easy to call them materialists; easy to say that they could never rise to Plato's disinterested love of truth and beauty. But is there not a great honesty in this refusal to divorce religion from hard fact? The Jews could not believe in a God who allowed the world to be misgoverned. Rather than that, they would try every conceivable explanation of the evil in the world. The sins of the fathers are visited on the children; the apparently righteous sufferer is a secret sinner; the wheels of God grind slowly—each of these explanations was tried in turn, and others too. At last certain new truths began to dawn upon them; that " whom the Lord loveth He chasteneth "; that vicarious suffering is the law of redemption; and, latest of all, that the righteous live for ever in fulness of joy. in God's presence. For history certainly does not countenance the older theodicy of the Jews, which they were so reluctant to surrender. Terrible acts of injustice frequently occur in this world, and, so far as we can see, are never redressed. And more than this. God does not always punish a nation by sending it adversity; more often He gives the oppressors their hearts' desire, and sends leanness withal into their soul. At the same time, we must not suppose that the laws of nature favour the violent and unjust. In the long run nothing fails like ill-gotten success; the wolf-nations have died because they became intolerably wolfish. If we look far enough, there is a nemesis upon national injustice, though it comes in a very different way from that which the Jews expected. After all, the Jews have stood by the graves of all their oppressors in turn. Their " survival-value " has proved to be greater than that of the Assyrians and Persians, and even of the Romans. So far, their hopes were justified; but what a vast amount of purifying they needed to make them true! And how tragically did their fanatical nationalism prevent them from understanding and accepting the call for which God had been training them since the days of Abraham!

Well, then, we may venture to assert that in the long run, and with many exceptions, honesty is the best policy. Is this cold comfort all that history, and Christianity, can give us, in the way of Hope for this life? No, we can do better than that. What was wrong with the Jewish theory of divine justice was that their standard of values was untrue. They over-estimated the good things of this world—all that class of things in which one man's gain is another man's loss. They were, as a people, indifferent to that wide range of intellectual and spiritual values, the understanding

of which was the imperishable glory of Athens. And, as
we have seen, they had not anticipated the revelation
of new moral values which Christianity first opened out
to mankind. Now these mental and moral possessions
are their own reward. They cannot, like earthly possessions, be taken away from us. For those who know what
they are worth, the world is a much brighter place than
for those who think that a man's life consisteth in the
abundance of the things which he possesseth. The man
whose " mind to him a kingdom is " does not complain
much of the injustices of life. Still less does the true
Christian complain. He has found the joy that no man
taketh from him. This world is not a bad place in his
eyes, because he finds it full of love and beauty and
wisdom. He knows that it is God's world, even though,
in sad times like this, it seems to be " full of darkness
and cruel habitations." Amid all the horrors of war
and strife he sees the pure gold of love and heroism and
devotion shining brightly.

These spiritual gifts are not and never will be given
to those who seek them for any ulterior end, even the
greatness of their country ; and they are held on a
precarious tenure unless they are based on the firm
acceptance of the Christian standard of values which is
the basis of Christian Hope. It is one of the paradoxes
of religion that though it makes the outward conditions
of human society happy and healthy, it does not aim
directly at these objects. The good Christian has
already ascended in heart and mind with Christ, and in
a real sense he " continually dwells " in the eternal and
spiritual world. This is the truth in the charge of

"otherworldliness" so often brought against Christianity.
The charge is true ; but it is otherworldliness which alone
can transform this world. This is the meaning of our
Lord's words about earthly cares. " Seek ye first the
Kingdom of God and His righteousness, and all these
things shall be added unto you." Surely our own
observation confirms this. Who are the happy and
hopeful people, who diffuse an atmosphere of joy and
courage and helpfulness around them ? Are they not
the men of prayer, the men of vision ? And is it not
people of this kind—women perhaps rather more often
than men—who really hand on the torch of Faith, Hope,
and Love, kindled in Galilee nearly two thousand years
ago and never more to be put out ? Such men and
women bring far more disciples to Christ than eloquent
preachers and great organisers. They make the world
a better place by being in it. Therefore we must say
fearlessly to the patriot, the social reformer, and the
moralist : set your affections on things above ; live as
much as you can in heaven with Christ ; you will help
on your schemes for the betterment of society most
effectively by doing so.

But we must not disguise from ourselves that God's
dealings with this world are still a very difficult problem.
After reading the Old Testament we have no right to
think that what perplexed the chosen people for so many
centuries will all be plain to us even with the New
Testament to guide us. There is a great deal of shallow
optimism which " heals too slightly " the wounds which
experience inflicts upon Faith and Hope. It is useless
to say, "God's in His heaven ; All's right with the world,"

when many things are obviously all wrong in the world. It is vain to argue, as Emerson does, that divine justice is an automatic self-adjusting machine, so that all get their deserts (not of course in a grossly material sense) in this life. Eminent literary men in the last century were too secure and comfortable to see what a rough place the world is for the majority of those who live in it. It was only after long travail of soul that the Jews learned their lesson ; we shall not learn ours by turning epigrams. Remember that complacent optimism, as well as pessimism, is treason against Hope. The world, as it is, is not good enough to be true. We ought not to be satisfied with it. " God has prepared some better thing." But it by no means follows that what God has prepared is what we should now choose. There may be heavy sorrows and disappointments in store for us ; if so, it will mean that our hopes need purifying.

In conclusion, then, the duty of Hope means a call to a deeper spiritual life, to a firmer faith in the Christian revelation and in the promises of God, and above all, perhaps, to an acceptance of " the offence of the Cross," that stern doctrine which is at the same time the basis of the most indomitable hopefulness that the world has seen. This world exists for the realisation in time of God's eternal purposes. Some of these are bound up with individual lives, for God intended each one of us to do and to be something ; others have a far wider scope, and require far more time for their fulfil- ment. The manifold evils in the world are allowed to exist because only through them can the greater good be brought into activity. This greater good is not any external achievement, but the love and heroism and self-sacrifice which the great conflict calls into play. We must try to return to the dauntless spirit of the early Christians. " Who shall separate us from the love of Christ ? Shall tribulation, or distress, or persecution, or famine, or nakedness, or peril, or the sword ? Nay, in all these things we are more than conquerors through Him that loved us." We have missed this note in modern Christian teaching ; now we need it. And let us remember, when we are inclined to be disheartened, that the private soldier is a poor judge of the fortunes of a great battle. There is a fine poem by Clough, a poet too much neglected in our generation, which expresses this thought :—

" Say not, the struggle nought availeth,
    The labour and the wounds are vain :
The enemy faints not, nor faileth,
    And as things have been, they remain.

If hopes were dupes, fears may be liars ;
    It may be, in yon smoke concealed,
Your comrades chase e'en now the fliers,
    And, but for you, possess the field.

For while the tired waves, vainly breaking,
    Seem here no painful inch to gain,
Far back, through creeks and inlets making,
    Comes silent, flooding in, the main.

And not by eastern windows only,
    When daylight comes, comes in the light ;
In front the sun climbs slow, how slowly,
    But westward, look, the land is bright."

CHAPTER V

JOY

LOVE, joy, peace, faith, hope, humility : these are the characteristic Christian ideas. Whenever these words threaten to drop out of our vocabulary, or are used with an unpleasant suspicion of unreality, cant, or affectation, we may be sure that we are losing the essence of the Christian spirit, and are falling back into paganism. It is an absolutely sure and scientific test. If we do not want the words which Christianity had to coin to express its new ideas, the reason must be that we have lost the ideas themselves.

Why did Christianity need a new word for *Joy ?* Had not the pagans pleasure in their lives ? Is classical literature less cheerful reading than the Fathers of the Church ?

Joy is one thing, and pleasure is another. Pleasure is an instrument contrived by nature to induce the individual to carry out nature's designs for the continuance of the race : it subserves the preservation and propagation of life. Pleasure gives us no guidance as to the direction in which the life of the race is moving. It is a bait, which nature keeps dangling before our eyes—that is all. I do not mean that the wise man will refuse to take the bait, as Schopenhauer tells us.

That is the pessimistic asceticism of Asia, not Christianity nor good sense. But without despising pleasure, we must distinguish it sharply from Christian joy. Pleasure is a transient feeling; it ceases with its own gratification, and if that is repeated often, it passes into satiety. It is pleasure, and not joy, as Keats unhappily says, " whose hand is ever on his lips, bidding adieu." Joy has an eternal quality; " no man taketh it from us."

Joy is the emotional experience which our kind Father in heaven has attached to the discharge of the most fundamental of all the higher activities—namely, those of inner growth and outer creativeness. Joy is the triumph of *life;* it is the sign that we are living our true life as spiritual beings. We are sent into the world to become something and to make something. The two are in practice so closely connected as to be almost inseparable. Our personality expands by creativeness, and creates spontaneously as it expands. Joy is the signal that we are spiritually alive and active. Wherever joy is, creation has been; and the richer the creation, the deeper the joy.

It is the chief message of the philosophy of the last thirty years—this emphasising of *life* as the supreme category. It is thoroughly in accordance with the best Christian teaching, and it helps us to understand more clearly than perhaps was possible in the past the meaning of Christian joy, and the truth to which it bears witness.

Let me give some examples of joy. Christ himself bids us to think of the young mother, who remembereth no more her anguish, for joy that a man is born into the world. To have been instrumental in creating a human being—to have fulfilled this sacred duty of handing on the torch of life—is a " joy in widest commonalty spread." It is quite different from pleasure ; for pain, not pleasure, attends the birth of children. It is the triumph of life, the pride of creation.

This is a woman's joy *par excellence*. A man's is generally connected with his work in life. It is the sense of hitting the mark, of success, in a worthy sense of the word. There are few purer sources of happiness than the consciousness of having actually made or produced something good of its kind. Whether the product be useful, or beautiful, it is the same. If it was worth doing, and if we have done it, or rather, are doing it, joy results. But the joy is greater in proportion to the spiritual value of the thing produced. A great work of art, or a great scientific discovery, gives greater joy to its maker than a work of merely technical or mechanical skill. And the fulfilment of the prophetic and priestly function of bringing a human soul to the knowledge of God and the service of man gives perhaps the deepest joy of all.

Those who have not known the joy of achievement often suppose that men are ambitious and covetous of external reward when they are really desirous only to create and to taste the joy that creation brings. A man does not as a rule care much for applause and recognition except when he is not quite sure that he is working on the right lines. When he is sure, as St. Paul was sure, it is a very small thing for him to be judged of man's judgment. St. Paul's joy is not touched by the opinions of other men about him and his work. If

E

they misrepresent and persecute him, it makes no difference. When he says to the Thessalonians, " Ye received the word in much affliction, with joy of the Holy Ghost " ; when he speaks of himself and his fellow-apostles as " sorrowful, yet alway rejoicing," he shows how much deeper a thing joy is than pleasure, and how independent it is of adventitious circumstances.

Joy was a characteristic of the Christian community so long as it was growing, expanding, and creating healthfully. The time came when the Church ceased to grow, except externally in wealth, power and prestige ; and these are mere outward adornments, or hampering burdens, very likely. They do not imply growth, or creativeness. The time came when dogmatism, tyranny, and ignorance strangled the free intellectual activity of the Church, and worldliness destroyed its moral fruitfulness. Then Joy spread her wings and flew away. The Christian graces care nothing for names and labels ; where the Spirit of the Lord is, there they abide, but not in great Churches that have forgotten Him. How little of Joy there is in the character of the religious bigot or fanatic, or in the prudent ecclesiastical statesman ! A show of cheerfulness they may cultivate, as they often do ; but it is like the crackling of thorns under a pot : we cannot mistake it for the joy of the Lord which is the strength of the true Christian.

God sent us into the world to create something, and to enrich our own personality in the process. In our wrestling with intractable material, we have to draw on what is *above* ourselves. We have to rely on God's help to make anything worth making. And in drawing upon this power above ourselves, we take this higher power *into* ourselves; we raise ourselves above ourselves. This is how creativeness and inner growth mutually condition each other.

I want you to think earnestly of the witness which Joy on the one hand, and its antithesis, Boredom, on the other, bear to the duty and happiness of creative work, that is to say, real work, on however small a scale. The happy people are those who are producing something; the bored people are those who are consuming much and producing nothing. If you want to see examples of the latter class, look in at the bow-window of a London Club in the morning, or at the carriages in Hyde Park towards the end of the season. While we are still on our probation, God punishes the useless by giving them pleasure without joy; and very wearisome they find it. We are all given the choice whether we will crawl or climb. Parasitism is open to us, if we like. Choose it, and pleasure, that apple of Sodom—may be yours; but you will wholly forfeit joy.

Boredom, then, is a certain sign that we are allowing our best faculties to rust in idleness. When people are bored, they generally look about for a new pleasure, or take a holiday. There is no greater mistake: what they want is some hard piece of work—some productive drudgery. Doctors are fond of sending their fashionable patients to take a rest-cure. In nine cases out of ten, a work-cure would do them far more good.

Boredom is not the only enemy of Joy; there is also mental depression. If Christianity made joy a moral

virtue, it must regard joylessness as a moral fault.   And
so it does.   St. Paul, you will remember, warns the
Corinthians against " the sorrow of the world," which
" worketh death."   The sorrow of the world is con-
trasted with godly sorrow, or repentance for sin.   The
medieval casuists studied this among other temptations ;
they enumerated its symptoms ;   and in its extreme
form branded it as one of the seven deadly sins, under
the name of *acedia*.   Acedia (sometimes "accidie" in old
English), is a compound of depression, sloth, and irri-
tability, which " plunges the whole man into a lazy
languor, and works in him a constant bitterness."   " This
rotten sin," says Chaucer, " maketh a man heavy,
wrathful, and raw."   " Thence cometh somnolence,
that is, a sluggy slumbering, which maketh a man
heavy and dull in body and soul ;   negligence or reck-
lessness that recketh of nothing whether he do it well
or badly ;   and idleness, that is at the gate of all harms."

It is an unfamiliar idea to us, that depression is so
morally dangerous as this.   But perhaps the old moralists
were right, though we should now make more allowance
for the state of the sinner's nerves and digestion.   But
what I want to emphasise is this.   Mental depression
is often the aching of an unused faculty.   It is a salutary
pain, warning us that there is something wrong with
our plan of life.   If we look on it in this way, it may
be a blessing in disguise.   You who suffer from it, look
on it as a driving force, which may be and should be
used to force your life forward.   Do not waste it ;   do
not let the millstone grind itself away for want of corn
to grind.   Do not brood ;   do not fret ;   but think the

matter out.   There is something in me which complains
and grumbles : what does it want ?   It wants to have
the joy of creation and achievement : what can I do to
satisfy this craving ?   If you will use your attacks of
depression in this way, they will drive you forward in
a way which is impossible to the bovine, contented
temperament, which takes life as it comes.   The man
who is often depressed generally has good stuff in him ;
but the danger of *acedia* is very near, and it is not a
pleasant vice, for ourselves or our neighbours.   Make
your depression a stepping stone to a richer joy ; that
is what God meant it to be ; that is why He sent it
to you.

In our attitude to things which are not in our power,
the Psalmist's advice is salutary, " Fret not thyself,
else shalt thou be moved to do evil."   We are not
responsible where we have no power, and we have the
Divine promise that all things shall work together for
good to those who love God.   God has all time to work
in, and fulfils Himself in many ways.   Joy will be ours,
in so far as we are genuinely interested in great ideas
outside ourselves.   When we have once crossed the
charmed circle and got outside ourselves, we shall soon
realise that all true joy has an eternal and Divine
source and goal.   We are immortal spirits, set to do
certain things in time ; were it not so, our lives would
lack any rational justification.   The joy of achievement
is the recognition of a task understood and done.   It
is done, and fit to take its place—however lowly a place
—in the eternal order.   So far, so good ; now for the
next task.   To do our duty in our own sphere, to try

to create something worth creating, as our life's work, is the way to understand what joy is in this life, and, by God's grace to earn the verdict : " Well done, good and faithful servant ; enter thou into the joy of thy Lord."

CHAPTER VI

A LIVING sacrifice. No maimed or crippled thing might be offered to God, by the Jewish law. If we would devote ourselves to God, we must see to it that we have a self to devote. Self-consecration is not a negative thing; it is a very positive thing. Just as rest can only be defined as unimpeded activity, so self-sacrifice is the supreme energy and assertion of the human will. It is not a living death, but a dying life, to which we pledge ourselves when we say, " Lo! I come to do Thy will, O God."

What we are matters much more than what we do or say. At the core of every man's soul, deeper even than consciousness, lies the hidden man of the heart who can hear God speak. And if in ourselves that inmost shrine is a temple of the Holy Ghost, our words and actions will show from whence they came. Deep calleth unto deep; and those whose hearts God has touched can find their way easily to the hearts of others. The soul may have wandered far from its true home; but when it meets one who has *been there*, who can bring it tidings of that dear and half-forgotten land, it will spring to meet him. Here is someone who knows;

he can tell me what I want to know. Ask yourselves,
Who are the people who have really helped me ? You
will find, I think, that they have been laymen more
often than clergymen, women perhaps more often than
men ; that the occasions have been most trivial, that
the words spoken and things done have been slight and
unpremeditated. They have been sidelights upon the
person's character, peeps into the inner life of one whom
God hides privily by His own presence from the pro-
voking of all men ; whose mind is kept in perfect peace
because it is stayed on God ; of one who sees God because
his heart is pure. It is the sudden sting of self-reproach,
the shame of the contrast, the longing to be like such an
one, to see things as he sees them, that sticks in a man's
mind, and sends him to his knees as soon as he is alone.
Sometimes when such a man or woman dies, we learn
for the first time, not without surprise, what he or she
has been to many. Such persons have laid up a rich
store of gratitude by being what God has helped them
to be. A character can never be refuted or ignored ;
disinterestedness is always interesting. Do you remember the striking words of Milton about the true poet ?—
words which need very slight changes to make them
fit the true Christian : " He who would not be frustrate
in his hope to write well in laudable things ought himself to be a true poem ; that is, a composition and
pattern of the best and honourablest things ; not pre-
suming to sing high praises of heroic men or famous
cities, unless he have in himself the experience and the
practice of all that is praise worthy." Even our blessed
Lord said in His high-priestly prayer, " For their sakes

I consecrate myself." Self-consecration is the most effectual way by which we can serve God in our generation. This is the way in which the torch has been handed on by the long succession of runners since the Gospel of Christ came into the world.

The indwelling Spirit of Christ radiates its benign influence as Life, as Light, and as Love. Christ is the eternal principle of life in all that lives. " That which came into being, in Him was Life, and the Life was the Light of men." He came " that we might have Life, and have it more abundantly." The call of Christ is the call to a more vivid, earnest, strenuous life. It has been said of a great man that he passed through the dream of life as one awake ; and that is what all Christians ought to do. " Now it is high time to awake out of sleep." Spiritual wakefulness means concentration of purpose. The world may be divided into those who have a purpose in life, and those who have none, or who fluctuate between several. Few things are more striking than the change which comes over even the outward appearance of a man or woman between youth and old age, according to whether he or she has or has not a fixed purpose which is being carried out day by day. The face of the man who has found his work shows, in each decade of his life until the failure of his powers, increasing strength and dignity, and even beauty ; while the man who lets himself drift shows in every line of his face that his will has been overpowered by disorderly impulses, or has simply abdicated. The portraits of good and great men at various ages, and the faces of those who are neither good nor great, are instructive in this way. For us concentration of purpose means, in St. Paul's words, bringing into captivity every thought to the obedience of Christ. This involves a steady watchfulness. It means that we are at all times to keep a check upon the thoughts that flow unbidden into our minds, not only vindictive, avaricious, impure thoughts—though he is a happy man who can say that none such ever knock loudly for admittance—but wasteful, idle thoughts which sometimes dig deep channels in our minds before we realise it, and depressing thoughts which only diminish our powers of good work. I do not mean, of course, that the bow must be always strung ; the wise man will waste many half-hours from time to time ; but he should, so to speak, obtain his own leave before doing so. Nor do I mean that we should run in blinkers, for fear of distracting ourselves from our main purpose. "All things are ours," so long as "we are Christ's." Wide interests are a condition of wisdom and helpfulness. But the main purpose should never be really forgotten.

We have, of course, to admit our limitations, some of which are serious, while others are not. What is called "a narrow sphere" does not matter much. A broad mind is not much cramped by a narrow sphere. Some of the noblest and loftiest lives have been led under the most meagre and depressing conditions. No ; it is our personal defects that hamper us ; our mental sluggishness and our want of sympathy ; yes, and the heavy burdens which we have to carry, in the sins which do most easily beset us. These are the chains with which we are tied and bound. But I think we are as much inclined to underrate our possibilities as to over-rate our achievements. The New Testament seems to encourage a more sanguine estimate of what we are good for, as well as a more severe estimate of what we are bad for, than most of us find it easy to accept. There is a distinct promise of a " newness of life " which we may hope for. St. Paul's words, " I die daily," are the most hopeful, the most optimistic view of life that has ever been propounded. They mean that by living through an infinite number of tiny choices, each involving the rejection of the lower possibility and the adoption of the higher, we may in truth get rid of the moral impediments which grieve us so acutely. They do really die and disappear. If we believe this we can put up with the other limitations. If we can grow up slowly in all things into the Head, even Christ, our personal disadvantages, whatever they may be, will come to seem to us something external, not spoiling our true life.

As Christ is our life, so He is also our light. And surely the light means, among other things, the open mind towards Divine things. We need not be afraid of losing our faith by facing all problems honestly, while our lives are on the right lines. But while our minds are shut we cannot help others in their difficulties. We are more likely to turn them away from Christianity. The shut mind is always ready to bring the ark of God into the camp when the Philistines threaten, or to do like the Chinese, who piled their best crockery on the rails to stop the first locomotive which ran in their country. The best thing I know that has been said about the relations of faith with knowledge or illumination is this short passage from Clement of Alexandria, who wrote about two hundred years after Christ : " It is not doubting, but believing, which is the foundation of knowledge. But Christ is both the foundation and the superstructure, with whom are the beginning and the end. The extreme points—faith and love—are not taught. But knowledge is entrusted to those who are worthy of it, and from it love beams forth, from light to light. For it is said, To him that hath shall be given ; to faith, knowledge is given ; to knowledge, love ; and to love, the inheritance. And this takes place whenever a man hangs on the Lord by faith, by knowledge, and by love, and ascends with him to where the God and Guardian of our faith and love dwelleth."

So we are led on to the third of St. John's great words : " God is love ; and he that dwelleth in love dwelleth in God, and God in him." And we are reminded again of the great motive of self-consecration. " For their sakes I consecrate myself." Few things are more futile than sentimental exhortations about love, without forming any clear idea of what we mean by it. To begin with, Christian love is not a maudlin sentiment, but the practical recognition of a plain fact involving a claim. The plain fact is that we are the children of God, who made us and cares for us, and members one of another, so closely bound together that if one member suffer all the members suffer with it. The characteristic Christian attitude towards the happiness and sorrow, the virtues and sins, of others is that we should feel them as if they were our own. The true Christian feels a natural pleasure in seeing others happy ; his sympathy with other people's troubles is equally spontaneous, because he feels as if they had fallen upon himself. The sight of goodness in others fills him with thankfulness ; he rejoices to see the grace of God at work. And when he is confronted with moral evil, his feelings are equally far removed from the half-cynical toleration of the man of the world and from the vindictive indignation of the mere moralist. His first feeling is not of anger, but of shame and sorrow, almost as if he had committed the wrong himself. Vindictive anger is most easily aroused when crime seems to have been successful. But the Christian is under no temptation to envy such success. Our Lord unquestionably owed His unique power of reclaiming sinners to His sympathy with them, to His recognition of something lovable in their personality, in spite of all the corruption of their lives. But this redeeming sympathy for sinners can be exercised only by those who have no sympathy whatever with their sins. Admission to redemptive work, which is the sign and fruit of redemption, is the reward of complete self-consecration. In minor degrees we can exercise this power, we can claim for ourselves this Divine privilege, but only in proportion as we have shut the door finally upon such temptations in ourselves.

It is thus plain that if we wish to render unto God reasonable service, we must begin by " taking heed to ourselves." We are all quite rightly immersed in external activities, and perhaps say that we have no time to think about our own souls. But we are never really too busy to pray, and there was never a time when the world needed true inward Christians more than it does now. The Churches, we are told, are on their trial. That may be; we, at any rate, are not sitting on the bench, nor does any human judgment matter much. To his own master each man standeth or falleth; and He that judgeth us is the Lord. But we shall serve our Church and our country best if we perform, day by day and hour by hour, those humble and simple acts of self-dedication which will build up in us "that mind which was also in Christ Jesus," and which will make our lives a silent witness to Him who brought Life and Light and Love into this sorrowful world.

CHAPTER VII

THE WORLD

" THE World " in our New Testament is a translation of two Greek words, one of which means " the Age," or " the existing world-order," while the other is used in all the senses of our English word. It may mean the whole universe ; or our earth ; or the sum of its human inhabitants. But it is also used in a special sense. It means (to quote Bishop Gore's definition) human society as it organises itself apart from God. It is in this sense that St. Paul bids us to use this world, but not to abuse it, or rather, not to use it to the full. It is in this sense that the devil is called the prince of this world, and boasts, at the Temptation of Christ, that he has the power over this world. It is in this sense that St. John exhorts us not to love the world, or the things that are in the world, which he sums up as the lust of the flesh, the lust of the eyes, and the pride of life. It is in this sense that the whole world is said to lie in wickedness, or in the wicked one, knowing neither Christ nor the true disciples of Christ.

The world in this sense is a co-operative society with limited liability, existing for purely secular and chiefly for selfish ends, some of which can only be realised by combined action, preying on the weakness of others, and exploiting their moral as well as physical and economic

weakness. If its victims are trampled on, or if they are
tempted to take part in iniquities the guilt of which is
spread and distributed over a large number of persons,
the world disclaims all responsibility. Like the Chief
Priests to the remorseful Judas, it says, " What is that
to us ? See thou to that." All who take part in
practical work, especially in political or semi-political
work, but also in business or commerce, know how
extremely difficult it is not to be caught in the toils
of this ubiquitous and intricate machinery ; they know
how difficult it is to win any sort of success without
soiling our hands and straining our consciences.

Against this tremendous system Christ, standing alone,
declared war, and committed His followers to a state
of war, with no promise of any end to it. He was
perfectly clear about it. " Marvel not, my brethren, if
the world hate you. If the world hate you, ye know
that it hated me before it hated you. If ye were of
the world, the world would love its own ; but because
ye are not of the world, but I have taken you out of
the world, therefore the world hateth you."

There is thus a vein of apparently deep pessimism
in the Gospel. Christians are, in this world, not only
strangers and pilgrims, but in a sense rebels against
the powers that be. And they must be prepared to
be treated as such. This declaration of war against
society is profoundly unwelcome to most of us, because
we have been deluded by the absurd catchword that
the voice of the people is the voice of God, which it
never has been since the voice of the people cried
" Crucify him, crucify him," and never will be. In

religion, too, the popular catchwords of complacent institutionalism, the so-called revival of the corporate idea, indicate on the whole a reversion to political and external religion, the very thing against which the Gospel declared relentless war. The tendency contains an element of truth, as I shall show presently; but *esprit de corps* aims at political power by political methods; it makes its appeal to men in masses; it shapes its policy by what are euphemistically called " human needs," which means popular prejudices. The truth is that, as the brilliant French writer Charles Pèguy (one of the victims of the war) said, there has always been a conflict between what he calls mysticism and politics. Every spiritual ideal is perverted and strangled when " the world " gets hold of it. The world is very clever; it likes to play with idealism and patronise it; that is the best way to draw its sting. The Florentines flattered Savonarola till they found that he meant business; then they burnt him. Organised religion, I regret to say, is often the executioner in these cases.

Real Christianity is a revolutionary idealism, which estranges conservatives because it is revolutionary, and the revolutionary because it is idealistic. At the same time, it sanctions and blesses the purest motives of both sides. It binds together the living present and the living past; it brings out of its treasure things new and old; old things which are ever new, and new things which were in the counsels of God before the world began. It proclaims equality, and counsels submission; it denounces luxury, and preaches contentment.

F

It increases immeasurably the world's stock of those values which the world does not care for.

But Christ proclaims not only war, but victory, and victory already won. " Be of good cheer ; I have overcome the world ! " This is a radical optimism, behind a superficial pessimism. Christ has overcome the world, for Himself and for us, by repudiating its authority, denying its standards, renouncing its rewards and calmly accepting its punishments. It is a victory won through suffering, but a complete victory. So St. Paul felt it. " O death, where is thy sting ? O grave, where is thy victory ? Thanks be to God, who giveth us the victory through our Lord Jesus Christ." " In all these things we are more than conquerors through him that loved us." " Our light affliction, which is but for a moment, worketh for us a far more exceeding and eternal weight of glory."

Of course this optimism rests on faith in eternal life. " We look not on the things that are seen, but on the things that are not seen. For the things that are seen are temporal, but the things that are not seen are eternal." In all true Christianity there is a deep though often latent conviction that this world of ours and all that it contains is something fleeting and unreal, at best a mere shadow of heaven. " All that is in the world, the lust of the flesh and the lust of the eyes and the pride of life, is not of the Father but is of the world. And the world passeth away and the lust thereof, but he that doeth the will of God abideth for ever." " Thou, Lord, in the beginning hast laid the foundation of the earth, and the heavens are the work

of thy hands. They shall perish, but thou shalt endure ;
yea, they all shall wax old as doth a garment ; and
as a vesture shalt thou fold them up and they shall be
changed ; but thou art the same, and thy years shall
not fail." The creation, as Goethe says, is the living
vesture of God ; He clothes Himself with it, sees it
wear out, and changes it. But the life of the Spirit
is indestructible. Shakespeare, with all the vividness
and intensity of his life in time, the keen and brilliant
life of a true son of the Renaissance in Elizabethan Eng-
land, felt as strongly as any cloistered saint that man
walketh in a vain shadow and disquieteth himself in
vain. In that wonderful scene at the end of the *Tempest*,
our great dramatist, it seems to me, for once lets
us see his own deepest self, and speaks to us through
the mouth of Prospero. Are not those words, which
we all know so well, the poet's own farewell to the
public ? Do we not see the great magician breaking
his staff, and saying good-bye to the world, before
retiring to those five mysterious and silent years between
his last play and his death ?

> " Be cheerful, sir ;
> Our revels now are ended. These our actors,
> As I foretold you, were all spirits, and
> Are melted into air, into thin air :
> And, like the baseless fabric of this vision,
> The cloud-capped towers, the gorgeous palaces,
> The solemn temples, the great globe itself,
> Yea, all which it inherit, shall dissolve,
> And like this insubstantial pageant faded
> Leave not a rack behind. We are such stuff
> As dreams are made on, and our little life
> Is rounded with a sleep."

" Be cheerful, sir." " Be of good cheer." For " though
the earthly house of this tabernacle be dissolved, we
have an house not made with hands, eternal in the
heavens." It was this knowledge that gave the early
Christians their undaunted courage. Justin Martyr,
writing to the Roman Emperor, says, " When you hear
that we look for a kingdom, you thoughtlessly suppose
that we mean a human kingdom, while we mean a
kingdom with God. This is evident from the fact that
when we are examined by you we confess that we are
Christians, though we know that death is the penalty
of confession. If it had been a human kingdom for
which we look, we should have denied to save our lives
and have endeavoured to remain undetected ; but
since our hopes do not rest upon the present order, we
do not heed those who take our lives, since in any case
we must die."

" Since our hopes do not rest upon the present order."
Is not this the charge so often brought against Christians
and Christianity, that their dreams of future bliss have
sucked all the life out of their earthly existence, so that
they do nothing to make this world better and promote
human progress ? The true answer, though it is not
a very popular one, is that the advance of civilisation
is in truth a sort of by-product of Christianity, not its
chief aim ; but we can appeal to history to support us
that this progress is most stable and genuine when it is
a by-product of a lofty and unworldly idealism. It is
not quite certain that Christianity either requires or
promises what we commonly mean by the progress of
humanity. Personally, I hope for it, as a matter of

reasonable faith, not so much from a study of history, which shows us life becoming ever more complex, but not much better or happier ; but rather because if the life of humanity has any unitary purpose and meaning in the mind of the Creator, it must, one would think, be intended to exhibit the same kind of advance which we can trace in individual lives which are well lived. But the progress of humanity, if there is any, is very slow and always precarious ; and it cannot go on for ever.

However, nothing can be more untrue than to suppose that the progress of the kingdom of God upon earth is not a matter of deep interest for true Christians. When Christ said to His disciples, " I have taken you out of the world," He certainly did not mean that He had taken them out of human society, with its duties and obligations. Heaven is not a far-away place to which we hope to go ; it is the presence of God in which we ought to live. The Christian soldier is no recreant, tarrying behind at the base and leaving others to go into the fighting line. And here comes the partial truth which, as I said, is mixed with much error in the popular cult of the corporate idea. We do need another co-operative society to combat the society of co-operative guilt which the New Testament calls the world. We must help each other to make the right life possible in society. This is the true office of the Church, the bonds of which Christ meant to be mutual love and willing service. In this sense, we do need to make Church life much more of a reality. In the first century, and still more in the second, while the persecutions exercised an artificial selection and kept the Church pure, there was a band of brethren of this kind, an anti-worldly society.

In the difficult times which are coming, Christians must above all things be true to their Master's teaching and methods. The results are not likely to be outwardly very striking ; but an earnest and steady witness to the Gospel of Christ, even on the part of a few persons, will be of immense value. For the world, even in the bad sense, is not wholly bad. It has a conscience, and it is not satisfied with itself. The hidden man of the heart in each man longs to play traitor to the prince of this world, and takes courage when he sees that he is not alone. So it is that a little leaven leaveneth the whole lump ; and so it is, too, that the sufferings of the innocent are the chief means by which the kingdom of Christ is set forward on this earth. " In the world ye shall have tribulation ; but be of good cheer, I have overcome the world."

CHAPTER VIII

BEREAVEMENT

A MICROBE, blindly following its instincts of self-preservation and reproduction, may destroy a life which would have benefited all mankind, or blight the happiness of loving hearts. The incompetence of politicians, the greed and vainglory of a very small minority of the population of Europe, have within the last ten years brought to a premature and violent death ten millions of young men, the flower of their nations and their hope for days to come. In face of this mystery, what are we to say or think?

Nature, to all appearance, destroys her children ruthlessly and aimlessly. But what is Nature? Is she, as a philosopher has lately said, "a blind unconscious giant," without malevolence but without intelligence, "careless of the single life," but hardly more careful of "the type"? Or, when we see an innocent and precious life struck down, with all its promise unfulfilled, are we tempted to say, "An enemy hath done this?"

We have heard this last theory too often lately. It is only too plausible, when we look at the state of the world around us. But I do not think we are even tempted to take it to ourselves when the sorrow of bereavement comes very near to us. Even if from us, as from the prophet Ezekiel, the desire of our eyes has been taken away by a stroke, so that for the remainder of our journey we must creep like a wounded bird with broken wing, I do not think that we accuse the enemy of souls as the author of our sorrow.

The doctrine that God is not omnipotent, but is struggling against obstacles, due either to the intractable nature of " Matter " (a very old solution), or to some malignant spiritual agency, has once more become popular in our time. It was the foundation of the old Persian religion, and of the Manichean heresy. It was held tentatively by John Stuart Mill, and is advocated by at least one prominent theologian in our Church. It is undoubtedly one method of justifying the ways of God to man. But I think that it is when we contemplate the affliction of others, rather than our own, that we murmur to ourselves, " A good God could not have sanctioned such cruelty." Or if we sometimes feel this in our own cases, it may be that we have substituted " le bon Dieu " of popular sentiment for the loving but wise and stern Father whom Christ taught us to fear as well as love. " Whom the Lord loveth He chasteneth." A generation which wishes for a religion without tears must find it difficult to adjust its beliefs to the teaching of the New Testament and to the facts of life.

I think that those who have had to bear this sorrow will agree with me that bereavement is the deepest initiation into the mysteries of human life, an initiation more searching and profound than even happy love. Love remembered and consecrated by grief belongs,

more clearly than the happy intercourse of friends, to
the eternal world ; it has proved itself stronger than
death.   Bereavement is the sharpest challenge to our
trust in God ; if faith can overcome this, there is no
mountain which it cannot remove.   And faith can
overcome it.   It brings the eternal world nearer to
us, and makes it seem more real.   It is not that we
look forward to anything remotely resembling Ezekiel's
vision of the valley of dry bones.   Still less could we
find any comfort from the pathetic illusions of modern
necromancy.   These fancies have nothing to do with
our hope of immortality, which would be in no way
strengthened by such support.   Rather does pure
affection, so remembered and so consecrated, carry us
beyond the bourne of time and place altogether.   It
transports us into a purer air, where all that has been,
is, and will be lives together, in its true being, meaning
and value before the throne of God.

There is no wilfulness or self-deception in this confidence.   It is God Himself, Who is Love, from Whom
we learn so to believe and so to hope.   Far less has been
revealed than we should like to know about the lot
of those who have left us ; and we are obliged to allow
the imagination to fill in pictures of those things which
it hath not entered into the heart of man to conceive.
We know very little, and we probably could not understand the truth if it were told to us.   But if we are
right in claiming for our judgments of value an authority
no less than we allow to our judgments of fact, which
come to us through the senses, we may assert with
confidence that the souls of the righteous are in the

hand of God, and that what is dear to Him will never be plucked out of the land of the living.

The frontispiece to this volume is a portrait of our little daughter, Margaret Paula, who entered into her rest on the night of Thursday in Holy Week, 1923. It is not congenial to me to tear aside the veil which secludes the sanctities of a happy home. There are some things about our little girl which I could not bring myself to say in English, or in prose, and which are therefore kept for the metrical dedication which I have written. But it has been my strange privilege, as I believe, to be the father of one of God's saints, a character as pure and beautiful as many which are recorded in the Church's roll of honour ; and I offer these pages which are to follow as a thank-offering for that precious gift, not without hope that my readers may be able, from this slight and meagre record, to realise something of the beauty and fragrance which accompanied that short but not imperfect life of eleven years.

We remember her first as a fine baby with a strong will of her own. But before long she became a fairy child, very graceful in her movements, very gentle and loving, and at times rather dreamy. She was only five years old when a friend with whom she was staying wrote : " Paula has an intense sweetness of disposition, so heavenly in her sweetness, gentleness and tenderness." This was the impression which she made increasingly on all who knew her, and it was the verdict of the nursery. On the day of her death I took her little brother on my knee, and told him that Paula was going to spend her Easter with Jesus Christ. After a good cry he said: "In all her long life—at least it seems a long life to me, though not to you—Paula has never made anybody angry; she has always made everybody happy." There was hardly ever any quarrelling in her presence.

She was taken ill eighteen months before she died, and during the whole of that time she had to live on a very low diet, without any of the dainties which children love. She bore the privation with a serenity and patience which astonished the doctors and nurses, who declared that they had never seen such a child. She continued to speak to us as if she expected to get well, but I think she really knew as much as we did. A few months before the end her little brother said to her when they were alone, "O Paula, I wish you would get better." The little boy was so much impressed by her answer that he repeated it to his mother. "No, Richard, you must not say that. God has spared me for a whole year to be with you all, and it has been the happiest year of my life." A little later, when she was no longer able to use her pencil and paintbox, she said to her mother: "I am the happiest little girl in all the world." It seemed to us that this happiness came from a vivid realisation that the everlasting arms were about her, and from a consciousness that the deep love which she felt for us all, including her kind doctor and nurse, was fully returned.

It was wonderful to see how quickly her character matured under the discipline of weakness. The words, "She is a real saint," were often spoken of her, and they seemed to us to be no more than the truth. On Palm

Sunday I repeated to her Milton's sonnet on his blindness ; and when I came to " They also serve who only stand and wait," I thought it right to say, " Paula, I should like you to remember that last line. You will never know how much you have done for all of us in this house, and for many others, simply by being what God has helped you to be." She was much pleased, and asked for the line again and again during the next two days.

Till the very end she was busy with her needle, making Easter presents for her parents, brothers and sister. During the last weeks she asked to discontinue her child-like practice of saying her prayers aloud to her mother or nurse. She said, " If you do not mind, I should like best to be quite alone with God."

It was on Tuesday in Holy Week that she said to her nurse : " Nannie, when Good Friday comes, I want you to take all my flowers and lay them with your own hands on the soldiers' monument at Westminster." The nurse said : " But I could not leave you, Paula. One of the maids can take the flowers if you wish to send them." She replied : " I can't help being glad that you think you ought not to leave me ; but I did mean that to be my Good Friday penance." The flowers were placed on the cenotaph, as she had desired ; but there were no more penances for her on Good Friday. She had already heard her Saviour say, " This day shalt thou be with me in Paradise."

The letters—there were nearly a thousand—which came in after her death showed how many outside the family had understood what she was. Her nurse wrote to Paula's mother : " I am trying to describe the beautiful and lovely character of dear little Paula. Never before have I met with so sweet and brave a nature. In spite of her illness, her last year has been wonderful. Being a Fairy Princess (as she really thought herself) she lived in a sweet imagination, loving all things beautiful, and doing things as a Princess should. On her fast days she often said, " I am a Princess, so I must not feel hungry." Apart from her fairy imagination, she loved everything that was good and holy, never forgetting her prayers or Bible and loving her little hymns, always mindful of that higher kingdom which was waiting for her. I like to think of those last few days. It was so wonderful to see her goodness and patience. Several times she said, " Nanna, I am so happy " ; although perhaps she did not know why, but I suppose it was just God's sweet peace in her heart. I am glad to have been with her for the last year of her life. She was so pleased to have a Nanna all to herself."

The hospital nurse also wrote : " She was so good and patient, filling her little corner of the world with a very wonderful fragrance. No one will forget her."

The little group of girls who initiated her into their Fairy Land game, and crowned her with a charming ceremony as " Princess Asphodel," loved her dearly. They made her a fairy dress for her " coronation," and this little scene will live in the memories of all who were present. One of them wrote : " She was one of the most lovely things I have ever known, and it has been a very wonderful year since I have known her, and the years will continue so, more and more lovely for her sake." And another : " What a wonderful fairy story is Paula's this week, beyond anything we could imagine for her. And how truly she is the Princess of the Spring. The daffodils must always be her flowers now ; she looked so like a pale daffodil herself, in that yellow velvet. But all beautiful things belong to Paula, and to know her is something to be thankful for."

Another, who is captain of an East End company of " Brownies," inducted her into that corps, and taught the poor children to honour her as the model Brownie. They came in their little russet uniforms to the funeral, and escorted the coffin as a guard of honour. Afterwards they came again to see her room. The " Brown Owl " wrote : " I have only known Paula since last May, but in that time I learnt to love and admire her more than anyone else I have ever known. I know that at least thirty-eight wee Brownies will truly miss their little friend, who to them (and to others) was a little Princess and an ideal Brownie."

Two or three other tributes may be quoted as representative of many more. " I always felt there was something so deeply attractive about Paula, something a little detached, a little mysterious, almost as if she knew something that was hidden from us—some secret too deep for revealing ; a little wistful too, as if she would have shared that secret if she could."

One who was present at the first part of the funeral service, in St. Paul's, says : " It was quite the most beautiful memorial service I have ever been to. It was all so simple, and yet so much dignity ; so little pomp and yet all so regal, such true feeling and true pathos on every side. One felt the beautiful spirit of that saint-like nature—the loving spirit of Paula—over everything. It was so wonderful, the tribute from the whole of that great city to Paula ; all the traffic stopped, the flowers, the silent tribute from the public, and the great quiet and peace. It was very wonderful." Another wrote : " I thought it so impressive to see that silent mass of bareheaded city men paying respect to that sweet frail little girl." It was indeed wonderful how the public had come to know about her. The omnibus conductors used to touch their hats as she drove past, in order to get an answering smile from the pale little face.

I hope my readers will not think that I have said too much about our little girl. There are, thank God, countless other beautiful child characters, and many may justly think that their own children are not less worthy of commemoration. But let what I have written be taken as a reverent tribute to the child nature, which our Saviour loved and bade us to imitate. At a time when so much of our literature is strangely blind to the glory and excellence of human nature at its best, I do not think that we can be blamed for making known what we have ourselves seen of the beauty of holiness in a short life, and for showing, as the letters which I have quoted and many others like them have shown, how many sweet natures there are in the world, swift to recognize and love that beauty when they see it in another. Some will I hope be reminded of children who, like our little daughter, have been lent them for a time and then taken home into the presence of the Lord of little children. For we ought to remember them, and " keep our memory green " for those sad but blessed experiences of our human lot. Some may perhaps have the same feeling that we have, that there may be a wonderful completeness in a life which only lasted a few years. " She, being made perfect in a short time, fulfilled a long time, for her soul was dear to the Lord."

PRINTED IN GREAT BRITAIN
AT THE BOWERING PRESS,
GEORGE STREET, PLYMOUTH